NEW DIMENSIONS.

WRITTEN BY

COLIN BOYNTON

ISBN: 978-1-9162837-0-1

COPYRIGHT : COLIN BOYNTON 2019

INDEX

1. FEELINGS
2. JUST PERFECT
3. YOU AND I
4. FREEDOM
5. EVER ON AND UP
6. YOU!
7. THIS IS IT!
8. ALONE
9. EYES DON'T LIE !
10. WHAT GOES AROUND
11. RUMOUR HAS IT
12. PERFECTION !
13. TO WALK AWAY
14. TOO LATE !!!
15. NO REGRETS
16. TIME PASSES
17. A LOVE LETTER TO LOVE
18. WINGS!
19. HEART BEAT
20. RHYTHMIC INSPIRATION
21. HIDDEN TRUTH
22. MY WISH
23. CH – CH – CH - CHANGES
24. HAVE YOU HEARD?
25. THE FASHION...

26. A THOUSAND AND ONE STARS
27. SECRETS
28. QUESTIONS
29. GRATITUDE
30. THE FIRST MOVE
31. LEGACY
32. CHAIN GANG
33. IMAGINATION
34. TIME TO DO THE RIGHT THING
35. MAYBE
36. WATCHING
37. FOLLOWING THE LEADER
38. NO TIME FOR REGRET
39. A LITTLE STORY
40. SUNRISE…SUNSET…
41. MY STORY
42. MIRROR IMAGE
43. TOP SECRET
44. IN SHADES OF GREEN
45. SO IT SEEMS
46. WHAT IS IT?
47. WHERE IS THE LOVE?
48. CLOUDS
49. HALF AND HALF
50. SOMEONE

51. JUST A LITTLE HELPS
52. SHOPPING
53. WINTER WASHING BLUES
54. DIFFERENCES
55. TIME
56. PEOPLE, PEOPLE EVERYWHERE
57. WHAT IF..?
58. THE LADIES WHO LUNCH
59. THIS IS ME
60. DEATH OF A HUNDRED YEARS
61. THE LIFT
62. STARS OF MEMORIES
63. YOUNG AND FREE
64. COLOURS BECOMING
65. CONNECTIONS
66. WHAT A WASTE
67. FINAL DECISION
68. I WHO HAVE NOTHING
69. I…
70. THE DANCER
71. YESTERDAY, TODAY, TOMORROW
72. IN YOUR CHAIR
73. APPRECIATION SOCIETY
74. WHAT I'VE GOT
75. MOBILE LIVES

1. FEELINGS

IT STARTED AGAIN
THE FEELING INSIDE
A FEELING SO STRONG
I JUST CANNOT HIDE
ENCOMPASSING ME
AND JUST TAKING HOLD
THIS FEELING SO STRONG
A FEELING SO OLD
GETTING MUCH BIGGER
EVERY DAY
A FEELING SO STRONG
IT TAKES ME AWAY
BACK TO A TIME
WHERE I ONCE FELT STRONG
THE FEELING REMINDS ME
OF WHERE I BELONG

2. JUST PERFECT

NO CLOUDS COULD SPOIL THE VIEW I SAW
NO RAIN COULD DAMP MY DAY
SO PERFECT WAS THE COUNTRYSIDE
IN EVERY SINGLE WAY
THE GRASS WAS GREEN, THE TREES IN LEAF
AND FLOWERS IN FULL BLOOM
IF ONLY I COULD BRING OUTDOORS
BACK IN TO MY ROOM
SO PERFECT WAS THE VIEW I SAW
A PICTURE POSTCARD SCENE
WAS EVERYWHERE AROUND ME NOW
AND EVERYWHERE I'D BEEN.

3. YOU AND I

I'M THE WRITER OF MY STORY
CREATOR IN MY LIFE
THE ONE WHO MAKES THE CHOICES
THROUGH TROUBLES AND THROUGH STRIFE

YOU MAKE YOUR OWN DECISIONS
AND CHOOSE YOUR PATH TO TAKE
IT WILL NOT ALL BE PERFECT
YOU'LL MAKE THE ODD MISTAKE

WE ALWAYS KNOW THE OUTCOME
OF CHOICES WE HAVE MADE
WHEN THE FUTURE HITS US
OUR LIVES BEHIND US LAID

I ONLY MAKE MY FUTURE
YOU CANNOT CHANGE YOUR PAST
WE LIVES OUR LIVES FROM DAY TO DAY
THAT CHANGE SO MUCH SO FAST

4. FREEDOM

WE'RE WALKING THE LINE
WE'VE CROSSED MANY TIMES
AND ONE DAY I KNOW WE'LL BE FREE
A BREAK FROM THE CHAINS
THE BONDS THAT BRING PAINS
AND ONE DAY WE ALL CAN BE FREE.

FREEDOM IS NOT JUST A DREAM THAT WE HAVE
IT'S SOMETHING THAT EVERYONE NEEDS
IT'S SOWN IN OUR MINDS AND GROWS IN OUR HEARTS
NOT FROM A HANDFUL OF SEEDS
A DREAM FOR A FUTURE, A FLIGHT FROM THE PAST
A CHANCE TO JUST SIMPLY BE
FREEDOM IS NOT JUST FOR SOMEBODY ELSE
IT'S SOMETHING FOR YOU AND FOR ME

WE'RE WALKING A LINE
TIME AFTER TIME
HEADED TO WHERE WE'LL BE FREE
ESCAPE FROM THE TIES
THAT DARKEN OUR SKIES
SOMEWHERE WHERE WE SIMPLY CAN BE

FREEDOM IS NOT JUST A WORD THAT WE HEAR
IT'S SOMETHING FOR EVERYONE
IT SHOULDN'T BE STOPPED AND SHOULDN'T BE BLOCKED
AND SO WE WILL KEEP FIGHTING ON
FIGHTING FOR FREEDOM FOR EVERYONE
FIGHTING TO GET BACK THE PEACE
UNTIL THERE IS FREEDOM FOR EVERYONE
THE TROUBLES WE HAVE WILL NOT CEASE

5. EVER ON AND UP

EVER ONWARD AND EVER UP
CLIMBING THE MOUNTAIN CALLED LIFE
EVERY STEP YOU CAREFULLY TAKE
AVOIDING THE TROUBLES AND STRIFE.
EVER ONWARDS AND EVER UP
WE ALL HAVE A JOURNEY TO TAKE
AND GROWING STRONGER DAY BY DAY
WITH EVERY DECISION WE MAKE.
EVER ONWARD AND EVER UP
FACING A FUTURE THAT'S BRIGHT
LOOKING BACK AT ALL THAT'S GONE
AND LEAVING IT WELL OUT OF SIGHT.
EVER ONWARD AND EVER UP
UNTIL WE ALL REACH OUR GOAL
AND IN THE END BE HAPPY AND TRUE
AT PEACE IN YOUR MIND AND YOUR SOUL.

6. YOU!

WHO'D HAVE THOUGHT YOU'D STEAL MY HEART
AND IN MY DREAMS YOU'D CREEP
TAKE AWAY MY LONELINESS
AT NIGHT WHILE I'M ASLEEP.
WHO'D THINK YOU'D BRING ME HAPPINESS
AND WIPE AWAY MY TEARS
BRING BACK JOY IN TO MY LIFE
AND EASE AWAY MY FEARS.
WHO'D HAVE THOUGHT THE CHANGE YOU'D MAKE
BY WHAT YOU DO AND SAY
AND NOW THAT I HAVE FOUND YOU
HERE IS WHERE YOU'LL STAY

7. THIS IS IT!

LET'S DANCE BY THE LIGHT OF THE MOON
AND WATCH AS STARS GO BY
CLIMB UP TO THE MOUNTAIN TOPS
BEFORE WE SAY GOODBYE
LET'S CROSS THE WIDEST RIVERS
AND SWIM FROM SHORE TO SHORE
WATCH THE CLOUDS GO DRIFTING BY
THIS AND SO MUCH MORE
LET'S LINGER IN THE BRIGHT SUNSHINE
AND COUNT THE MINUTES BY
LAY DOWN IN THE GREENEST GRASS
TOUCH THE BLUEST SKY
WE'LL WALK THE LINE FROM HERE TO THERE
ACROSS THE BURNING SAND
AND BRAVE THE WILDEST STORMS THERE ARE
COVERING THIS LAND
WE'LL DANCE AGAIN ONCE MORE MY FRIEND
SMILE AND GIVE A SIGH
AND WHEN WE REACH OUR JOURNEYS END
WE'LL SAY A FOND GOODBYE.

8. ALONE.

OUT FOR A WALK
ON A BRIGHT SUMMERS DAY
WALKING ALONE
IN MY OWN WAY
THE SUN IN MY EYES
THE WIND IN MY HAIR
WALKING THE FIELDS
WITHOUT ANY CARE
KICKING ALONG
DOWN BY A STREAM
MY MIND FAR AWAY
LIKE IN A DREAM
ENJOYING THE PEACE
ENJOYING THE QUIET
KNOWING THE REAL WORLD
IS WELL OUT OF SIGHT
WATCHING THE BIRDS
WATCHING THE BEES
LOOKING AT FLOWERS
AND LOOKING AT TREES
WANTING TO STAY
FOREVER AND MORE
HERE IN THIS BEAUTIFUL PLACE
I ADORE.

9. EYES DON'T LIE !

YOUR EYES THEY TELL THE STORY
OF WHAT YOU'RE GOING THROUGH
THEY SHARE YOUR JOYS AND SORROWS
AND EVERYTHING YOU DO
YOU CANNOT KEEP A SECRET
YOU CANNOT TELL A LIE
THEY'LL SHOW WHAT YOU HAVE HIDDEN
AND DO NOT EVEN TRY
YOUR EYES WILL TELL THE WHOLE WORLD
ALL THEY CAN OF YOU
REVEALING ALL YOUR FEELINGS
OF WHAT YOU'RE GOING THROUGH
SHOWING EVERYTHING THEY CAN
THEY'RE NEVER TELLING LIES
AND HOLDING NOTHING BACK AT ALL
THE TRUTH LIES IN YOUR EYES

10. WHAT GOES AROUND

IT SEEMS I'M ALWAYS STRIVING
TO BE THE BEST I CAN
DO THE BEST FOR EVERYONE
AND BE A DECENT MAN
BUT THINGS AREN'T ALWAYS SIMPLE
I NEED A HELPING HAND
SOMEONE WHO WILL LOOK AT ME
AND SAY I'M DOING GRAND
I KNOW I'M NOT THE ONLY ONE
WHO SOMETIMES FEELS THIS WAY
THERE'S OTHERS WHO WILL FEEL IT
TOMORROW OR TODAY
SO SPARE A SIMPLE LITTLE THOUGHT
BE KIND TO ALL YOU MEET
FOR SOME OF THOSE SAD PEOPLE
MAY BE UPON THE STREET
AND ONE DAY THAT SAD PERSON
MAY HAPPEN TO BE YOU
A PERSON MAY WALK RIGHT ON UP
AND KNOW JUST WHAT TO DO
IT COULD BE JUST A STRANGER
OR MIGHT EVEN BE ME
WHAT GOES AROUND WILL COME AROUND
SO SIMPLE AND IT'S FREE

11. RUMOUR HAS IT.

ISN'T IT AMAZING
THE STORIES THAT YOU HEAR
TALES OF THIS AND TALES OF THAT
COMING TO MY EAR
BUT I'M THE ONLY PERSON
WHO KNOWS JUST WHAT IS TRUE
AND I'M THE ONLY PERSON
WHO KNOWS JUST WHAT TO DO
I KNOW WHAT'S TRUTH OR RUMOUR
AND I'M NOT LETTING ON
LET THE RUMOURS FLY AROUND
I KNOW WHAT'S RIGHT OR WRONG
I DO NOT HAVE TO TELL THEM
I DON'T HAVE TO DISCLOSE
ALL I'LL DO IS WEAR A SMILE
AND FINGER TO MY NOSE.

IT'S MY BUSINESS!!!
NOT THEIRS!!!

12. PERFECTION !

IF MY HEART COULD
TAKE WITH ME
THE SIGHT THAT BOTH
MY EYES CAN SEE
I'D BE HAPPY
I'D HAVE PEACE
AND NEEDING NOTHING
MORE TO PLEASE
A COUNTRY VIEW
A SINGING BIRD
AND NOTHING MORE
TO BE HEARD
I HAVE NO WORRY
AND NO CARE
AS I SIT HERE
IN THIS CHAIR
IN THE SUN
AT END OF DAY
RESTING IN
THE PERFECT WAY!

13. TO WALK AWAY

DO YOU LISTEN TO ME?
CAN YOU HEAR MY VOICE?
ARE THEY WORDS YOU UNDERSTAND
OR IS IT JUST A NOISE?
DO YOU HEAR THE THINGS I SAY
CAN YOU HEAR EACH WORD?
IT'S LIKE YOUR PAYING NO ATTENTION
LIKE YOU NEVER HEARD
I TRY TO MAKE IT SIMPLE
SO YOU MIGHT UNDERSTAND
MY WORDS ARE CLEAR AND EASY
NOTHING VERY GRAND
IF YOU DON'T WANT TO LISTEN
TO WHAT I HAVE TO SAY
I'LL TURN MY BACK UPON YOU
AND SIMPLY WALK AWAY.

14. TOO LATE!!!

ARE WE DESTROYING
THE WORLD THAT WE KNOW
CUTTING DOWN TREES
AS FAST AS THEY GROW
POLLUTING THE WATERS
THE GROUND AND THE AIR
DESTROYING THE EARTH
THAT'S OURS TO SHARE
KILLING EACH OTHER
WITH POISONS AND GAS
DUST THAT IS TOXIC
FALLING EN – MASSE
DESTROYING ALL NATURE
BOTH GREAT AND SMALL
NOT SEEING OR CARING
NOT WORRIED AT ALL
ONE DAY IN THE FUTURE
WHEN IT IS TOO LATE
WE'LL MOURN THE DESTRUCTION
BY MAN AND HIS MATE
WITH NO FOOD TO EAT
AND NOTHING TO DRINK
TOO LATE TO STOP
AND TOO LATE TO THINK.

15. NO REGRETS

WE'RE ONLY GIVEN - JUST ONE CHANCE
TO LIVE OUR LIVES - IN THIS DANCE
TAKE IT SLOWLY - DAY BY DAY
STEP BY STEP - ALONG THE WAY
NO ONE'S PERFECT - NOTHING'S PURE
WE MAKE MISTAKES - THAT I'M SURE
SAY YOU'RE SORRY - IF YOU'RE WRONG
THIS WILL ONLY - MAKE YOU STRONG
GROW IN STRENGTH - GROW IN TIME
TAKE WHAT'S YOURS - IS NO CRIME
MAKE THE MOST - MOVING ON
TAKE THE CHANCE - BEFORE IT'S GONE
WE ONLY GET - ONE CHANCE TO LIVE
DO YOUR BEST - WITH TAKE AND GIVE
WITH NO REGRETS - WHEN YOU'RE THROUGH
WITH NOTHING LEFT - FOR YOU TO DO
AND KNOW YOU'VE DONE - YOUR VERY BEST
WHEN IT'S TIME - FOR YOU TO REST

16. TIME PASSES

LOOKING BACK AT WHAT WE HAD
AT WHAT HAS BEEN AND GONE
TIME HAS PASSED TOO QUICKLY
AND DIDN'T TAKE TOO LONG
MOONLIT NIGHTS AND STARLIT SKIES
RAINY DAYS OR SUN
TIME HAS PASSED TO QUICKLY
WITH ALL WE'VE SEEN AND DONE
GROWING UP AND GROWING OLD
WITH FEELINGS JUST THE SAME
TIME HAS PASSED TOO QUICKLY
CHANGED IN ALL BUT NAME
LOOKING FORWARD LOOKING BACK
PLANS WE'VE MADE OR MAKE
TIME HAS PASSED TO QUICKLY
IT'S OURS JUST TO TAKE
LIFE IS THERE FOR LIVING
MAKE IT WHILE YOU CAN
TIME IT PASSES QUICKLY
AND WAITS FOR NOT ONE MAN.

17. A LOVE LETTER TO LOVE

MEETING FOR THE FIRST TIME
YOU TURNED MY WORLD AROUND
YOUR SMILE IT SPOKE A THOUSAND WORDS
AND NEVER MADE A SOUND
OUR TWO HEARTS JUST COLLIDED
AND SPARKS LIT UP THE SKY
HAPPINESS CAME BURSTING THROUGH
TO MAKE THE DARK DAYS FLY
MY HEART JUST STARTED SKIPPING
AND MISSED A BEAT OR TWO
FROM THE VERY MOMENT
THAT YOU CAME IN TO VIEW
I WANT TO SHARE EACH MOMENT
SPEND EVERY DAY WITH YOU
YOU GAVE MY HEART ANOTHER CHANCE
AND MADE IT FEEL LIKE NEW
I DON'T KNOW HOW IT HAPPENED
BUT LOOK WHAT YOU HAVE DONE
CHASED MY DARK CLOUDS FAR AWAY
AND BROUGHT ME BACK THE SUN
TO HAVE ANOTHER CHANCE AT LOVE
AND HAPPINESS ONCE MORE
WAS MORE THAN I HAD DREAMED OF
THERE'S ONE THING I AM SURE
YOU'VE GIVEN ME NEW MEANING
AND GAVE MY LIFE A SHOVE
WITH ALL YOUR CARE AND TENDERNESS
YOU'VE GIVEN ME NEW LOVE.

18. WINGS!

I SPREAD MY WINGS
AND NOW I FLY
WATCH ME SOAR
AND TOUCH THE SKY
I HAVE NO LIMITS
HAVE NO CHAINS
SOARING HERE
NO ACHES OR PAINS
FLYING HIGHER
GLIDING LOW
FALLING FAST
AND RISING SLOW
FLY BY DAY
REST BY NIGHT
OUT OF VIEW
THEN BACK IN SIGHT
OVER VALLEY
THROUGH THE TREES
IN THE SUN
AND ON A BREEZE
OVER HILLS
AND OVER DALES
WINGS OUTSPREAD
A PAIR OF SAILS
A SILENT WHISPER
NEVER HEARD
THE OPEN WINGS
OF A BIRD.

19. HEART BEAT

WHEN I SIT VERY QUIET
THEN I CAN HEAR
THE SOUND OF YOUR HEART BEAT
LOUD AND NEAR
IT'S BEATING FOR YOU
AND IT'S BEATING FOR ME
THE RHYTHM OF LIFE
SO STRONG AND SO FREE
A MUSICAL RHYTHM
THAT I LIKE TO HEAR
MY HEAD ON YOUR CHEST
THE RHYTHM IS CLEAR
BEATING IN TIME
MY HEART BEATS TOO
THE RHYTHM OF LOVE
JUST FOR YOU.

20. RHYTHMIC INSPIRATION

HERE IS INSPIRATION
JUST KNOCKING AT MY DOOR
BRINGING ME A THOUSAND WORDS
AND VERY MANY MORE
BRINGING ME IDEAS
THINGS TO WRITE ABOUT
THOUGHTS THAT COME IN TO MY HEAD
I HAVE TO LET THEM OUT
WORDS UPON THE PAPER
AND WORDS THAT COME IN RHYME
WRITING OUT A PICTURE
EACH AND EVERY TIME
HERE COMES INSPIRATION
TO HIT ME ONCE AGAIN
GIVING ME IDEAS
'BOUT SUNSHINE AND 'BOUT RAIN
WORDS OF LOVE AND ROMANCE
WAITING TO BE TOLD
A STORY THAT IS OLD AS TIME
YET NEVER GROWING OLD
I'M WRITING OUT A STORY
IN RHYTHM ALL THE TIME
WORDS JUST FLOW ON TO THE PAGE
A STORY WROTE IN RHYME.

21. HIDDEN TRUTH

WE ALL THOUGHT THAT HE WAS FINE
GETTING ON MOST ALL THE TIME
WITH A SMILE UPON HIS FACE
EACH AND EVERY DAY.
NO ONE SAW THE PAIN INSIDE
SOMETHING HE WOULD ALWAYS HIDE
HIDDEN BY THE SMILE HE WORE
AND WENT UPON HIS WAY
KIND AND CARING, THOUGHTFUL TOO
BUT NO ONE EVER REALLY KNEW
THE JOYOUS SIDE THAT HE SHOWED
WAS ONLY THERE BY DAY
EACH NIGHT THE SMILE WAS SOON REPLACED
BY THE SADNESS THAT HE FACED
HE NEVER EVEN SHOWED THE WORLD
AND DIDN'T EVEN SAY
WE WATCHED, WE SPOKE, WE SAID HELLO
HOW VERY LITTLE DID WE KNOW
JUST WHAT IT WAS THAT HE WENT THROUGH
EACH AND EVERY DAY
HELPING OTHERS WHEN HE COULD
KNOWN FOR ALWAYS DOING GOOD
NEVER STOPPING FOR HIS THANKS
AND WENT UPON HIS WAY
THE HAPPY MAN THAT WE ALL SAW
SLIPPING IN AND OUT HIS DOOR
WITH HIS BRIGHT AND CHEERFUL FACE
WAS ONLY THERE BY DAY
THEN ON THE DAY HE WASN'T THERE
DID WE BOTHER DID WE CARE
WE DIDN'T EVEN SPEAK OF SADNESS
AND DIDN'T EVEN SAY.

22. MY WISH

I WISH THE WORLD COULD LIVE IN PEACE
WITH NO MORE GRIEF AND PAIN
I WISH THE WORLD COULD DRY ITS TEARS
THAT FALL JUST LIKE THE RAIN
TO LIVE IN COMPLETE HARMONY
IS WHAT I WISH MANKIND
IF ONLY WE COULD SEE THE HURT
AND NOT BE QUITE SO BLIND
BE KIND TO ONE ANOTHER
AND SHOW EACH OTHER CARE
TOGETHER AS WE LIVE OUR LIVES
THERE'S LOVE ENOUGH TO SHARE

23. CH – CH – CH – CHANGES

I'M DRAGGED IN TO THE 21ST
A CENTURY OF CHANGE
I DON'T KNOW WHAT IS HAPPENING
IT ALL SEEMS VERY STRANGE
AND JUST WHEN I AM CATCHING UP
THINGS MOVE ON AGAIN
I TRY TO UNDERSTAND THEM
BUT IT JUST DEFEATS MY BRAIN
IF SOMEONE COULD EXPLAIN TO ME
OR SHOW ME HOW IT'S DONE
I MIGHT JUST GET TO UNDERSTAND
THE CHANGES AS THEY COME
WHY AM I SO FAR BEHIND?
AND WHY AM I SO SLOW?
I TRY TO CATCH THE PRESENT TIME
BEFORE IT STARTS TO GO
PERHAPS I SHOULD JUST GIVE IN
AND LET THE WORLD GO BY
BUT PEOPLE SAY I SHOULD TRY MORE
AND I JUST ASK THEM "WHY?"

24. HAVE YOU HEARD?

RUMOURS ARE RUMOURS
AND NOT ALWAYS TRUE
AMAZING WHAT PEOPLE
WILL SAY ABOUT YOU
SOME PEOPLE BELIEVE THEM
AND OTHERS IGNORE
YOU KNOW THE RUMOURS
YOU'VE HEARD THEM BEFORE
SOMEONE TELLS A STORY
THAT SOMEONE BELIEVES
AND THE LIE OF THE RUMOUR
JUST NEVER LEAVES
YOU KNOW THE RUMOURS
AND YOU KNOW WHAT'S TRUE
DESPITE OF WHAT SOMEONE
MIGHT SAY ABOUT YOU
THE RUMOUR THAT'S STARTED
AND GOES ON AND ON
CAN KEEP GETTING BIGGER
BEFORE IT IS GONE
BUT THEN IN THE END
DO YOU REALLY CARE
THE RUMOUR'S A STORY
THAT'S NOT REALLY THERE

25. THE FASHION...

TELL ME, TELL ME, TELL ME
WHAT IT IS YOU DO
WHAT IT IS THAT MAKES YOU TICK
AND HOW IS IT YOU GREW
HOW IS IT YOU GOT SO BIG
DID THINGS GET OUT OF HAND
AND HOW COME YOU'RE SO POPULAR
ALL ACROSS THE LAND
HOW IS IT YOU GOT SO BIG
YOU STARTED OUT SO SMALL
I DO NOT UNDERSTAND IT
IT MAKES NO SENSE AT ALL
WHY DO PEOPLE TAKE YOU IN
AND WANT SO MUCH OF YOU
I JUST DON'T UNDERSTAND IT
THERE'S NOTHING THAT YOU DO
TELL ME, TELL ME, TELL ME
HOW YOU GOT SO GRAND
WILL IT LAST FOR VERY LONG
WAS ANY OF THIS PLANNED
ARE YOU JUST A PASSING CRAZE
IS THIS JUST THE WAY
WILL ALL OF THIS SUCCESS SOON END
AND THEN YOU'VE HAD YOUR DAY.

26. A THOUSAND AND ONE STARS

A THOUSAND STARS ARE SHINING
IN THE SKY TONIGHT
THERE ARE NO CLOUDS TO DIM THE VIEW
THE MOON IS SHINING BRIGHT
I WISH UPON A SHOOTING STAR
THAT SWEEPS ACROSS THE SKY
AND THEN I WATCH ANOTHER ONE
AS IT PASSES BY
SWEEPING 'CROSS THE NIGHT TIME SKY
THEN FALLING OUT OF VIEW
I SIT AND WATCH AND WONDER
WITH NOTHING ELSE TO DO
A NIGHT TIME CHILL BEGINS TO FALL
THE MINUTES TICK AROUND
SILENTLY I SIT THERE
I DO NOT HEAR A SOUND
I COUNT THE STARS UP IN THE SKY
MY EYES BEGIN TO CLOSE
I SOON BEGIN TO FALL INTO
A VERY PEACEFUL DOZE.

27. SECRETS

SOMETIMES I WILL WANDER
BACK THROUGH THE YEARS
HEARING THE SOUNDS
THAT NO ONE ELSE HEARS
VISITING PEOPLE
AND PLACES I'VE KNOWN
SOME ARE THE SAME
AND OTHERS HAVE GROWN
AND NO ONE ELSE KNOWS
JUST HOW I FEEL
SEEING AND HEARING
THINGS THAT AREN'T REAL
THINGS THAT ARE ONLY
THERE IN MY MIND
THE THINGS THAT ARE MEMORIES
ARE ALL THAT I FIND

28. QUESTIONS

WHAT IS IT THAT KEEPS THE WORLD
SPINNING ROUND AND ROUND
AND HOW IS IT THAT GRAVITY
MAKES THINGS FALL TO THE GROUND
WHAT IS IT THAT MAKES THE SEAS
KEEP WASHING TO THE SHORE
DOES GRAVITY KEEP PULLING THINGS
DOWN TO THE OCEAN FLOOR
WHY DOES DAY TURN IN TO NIGHT
AND THEN NIGHT IN TO DAY
WE SEE THE SUN RISE THEN IT SETS
BUT WHY IS IT THIS WAY
WHAT KEEPS THE CLOUDS UP IN THE SKY
WHAT MAKES THE FOUR WINDS BLOW
WHAT MAKES THE RAIN START FALLING
DOES ANYBODY KNOW
WHY HAS MAN JUST GOT TWO ARMS
AND BIRDS HAVE FEATHERED WINGS
MOST ANIMALS HAVE GOT FOUR LEGS
I'VE QUESTIONED ALL THESE THINGS
I'VE ASKED A LOT OF QUESTIONS
AND STILL HAVE MANY MORE
I NEVER GET THE ANSWERS
I'M NO WISER THAN BEFORE

29. GRATITUDE.

WHEN I THINK WHAT MIGHT HAVE BEEN
I GIVE A THANKFUL THOUGHT
AND WHEN I SEE WHERE I AM NOW
I SEE WHAT I'VE BEEN TAUGHT
I COULD BE WITH THE DOWN AND OUT
I COULD BE ON THE STREET
BUT I HAVE CLOTHES UPON MY BACK
AND SHOES UPON MY FEET
I COULD BE BEGGING JUST TO LIVE
TO BUY MYSELF SOME FOOD
I'VE GOT THE WATER IN MY GLASS
WHICH TASTES SO VERY GOOD
I HAVE A ROOF ABOVE MY HEAD
I HAVE SOMEWHERE TO REST
SO WHY WHEN THINGS GO VERY WRONG
IT FEELS JUST LIKE A TEST
I SHOULD BE VERY GRATEFUL
FOR ALL THE THINGS I'VE GOT
THERE'S SOMEONE LIVING OUT THERE
WHO DOESN'T HAVE A LOT
I AM A HEALTHY BEING
AND GET THE HELP I NEED
I AM VERY LUCKY
I KNOW HOW TO SUCCEED
I'VE BEEN DOWN BUT NOT QUITE OUT
AND GOT BACK ON MY FEET
I COULD HAVE STAYED THERE ON THE FLOOR
AND JUST ADMIT DEFEAT
IT ISN'T VERY EASY
YOU NEED A HELPING HAND
NOT EVERYONE IS WILLING
TO HELP OR UNDERSTAND
SO SPARE A THOUGHT FOR THOSE POOR SOULS
CRYING OUT TO YOU
LISTEN TO THEIR VOICES
AND SEE WHAT YOU CAN DO

30. THE FIRST MOVE

PEOPLE IN GLASS HOUSES
THEY SHOULD NOT THROW THE STONES
AND THINGS THEY SAY ABOUT ME
WILL NOT BREAK MY BONES
AND WHEN YOU POINT YOUR FINGER
TAKE A LOOK AND SEE
THEN ASK YOURSELF THE QUESTION
OF WHY YOU POINT AT ME
CAN YOU MAKE THE FIRST MOVE
ARE YOU SO PURE AND FREE
TAKE A LOOK AT YOURSELF
BEFORE YOU LOOK AT ME

31. LEGACY

THIS IS THE WORLD CREATED
BUILT FOR ME AND YOU
AND WE GO ON CREATING
FOR THE FUTURE TOO
WE LEAVE BEHIND A LEGACY
THE THINGS THAT WE HAVE DONE
ALL WE HAVE CREATED
WE LEAVE FOR EVERYONE
AND FUTURE GENERATIONS
WILL KEEP ON BUILDING TOO
WE'LL NEVER STOP CREATING
IT'S WHAT WE'LL ALWAYS DO
WE'VE DONE IT SINCE THE DAWN OF TIME
WE'RE DOING IT TODAY
WE'LL DO IT IN THE FUTURE
CREATING ALL THE WAY
WE MAY NOT ALWAYS LIKE THE THINGS
THAT MAN HAS BUILT OR DONE
BUT ONCE THINGS ARE CREATED
WE HAVE TO JUST MOVE ON
WE HAVE TO LIVE WITH OUR MISTAKES
AND OUR SUCCESSES TOO
IN THIS WORLD THAT WE CREATE
AND MAKE FOR ME AND YOU

32. CHAIN GANG

IF WALLS WERE BUILT TO KEEP US IN
THEN WHAT WILL KEEP US OUT
WITH VOICES HUSHED IN SILENCE
DOES ANYBODY SHOUT
VOICES IN THE WILDERNESS
VOICES NEVER HEARD
WE STRUGGLE TO GET OUT AGAIN
WHERE NO ONE EVER CARED
A STRUGGLE 'GAINST THE CURRENT
A STRUGGLE 'GAINST THE FLOW
PEOPLE MARCHING ONE WAY
BUT NOT THE WAY TO GO
WE WANT OUR INDEPENDENCE
WE'RE WANTING TO BE FREE
WE FOLLOW ONE ANOTHER
IS THAT THE WAY TO BE
BREAK THE CHAINS THAT BIND YOU
LET YOUR MIND BE FREE
BE THE PERSON WHO YOU ARE
AND WHO YOU WANT TO BE
FIND YOUR OWN DIRECTION
BE TRUE UNTO YOURSELF
IT'S TIME TO LIVE THE LIFE YOU WANT
SO STEP DOWN OFF THE SHELF

33. IMAGINATION!

IS WHAT I FACE
IN FRONT OF ME
A LIGHTING TRICK
REALITY?
THE REACHING HAND
A GRINNING FACE
THAT DISAPPEARS
WITHOUT A TRACE
THE HAUNTING LAUGH
THE FRIGHTENED SCREAM
IS IT REAL
OR JUST A DREAM
THE GHOSTLY SHADOW
OUT OF SHAPE
COMES AND GOES
I CAN'T ESCAPE
IN MY MIND
AND IN MY WAY
THERE AT NIGHT
GONE BY DAY
IT FOLLOWS ME
AND HAUNTS MY MIND
YET WHEN I LOOK
I CANNOT FIND
THE HEAVY STEP
THE QUIET SOUND
OF SOMEONE BREATHING
NEAR AROUND
AND THEN I HEAR
ANOTHER NOISE
SOUNDING LIKE
ANOTHER VOICE
SINGING LOUD
AND SINGING CLEAR
SOUNDING GOOD
TO MY EAR
IS THAT ME
OR IS IT YOU
IT'S NOT SOMETHING
THAT I DO

IMAGINATION ! (CONT...)

I'M VERY GOOD
UNTIL I FIND
THAT IT'S ONLY
IN MY MIND
I TAKE A BOW
AND BACK AWAY
TO FACE THE TRUTH
IN LIGHT OF DAY
SOMETHING MOVED
SMALL AND BLACK
MOVED AWAY
AND THEN CAME BACK
ALL OF THIS
AND SO MUCH MORE
IS WAITING JUST
OUTSIDE MY DOOR
IS IT REAL
OR IN MY MIND
IMAGINATION
SO UNKIND
IT FRIGHTENS ME
CAN SCARE ME SO
AND OFTEN I'VE
NOWHERE TO GO
I CAN'T ESCAPE
CAN'T GET AWAY
IT'S WITH ME NIGHT
AND WITH ME DAY
IT'S ONLY TRICKS
THAT'S PLAYED ON ME
BY MY OWN MIND
THAT I SEE.

34. TIME TO DO THE RIGHT THING

IF I SAID I'M SORRY
WHAT WOULD YOU SAY TO ME
COULD YOU LOOK ME IN THE FACE
AND SEE THE THINGS I SEE
AND IF I CAN FORGIVE YOU
CAN YOU DO THE SAME
DO NOT HOLD OR BARE A GRUDGE
THIS LIFE IS NOT A GAME
AND IF I SAID I LOVE YOU
I WONDER WHAT YOU'D SAY
COULD YOU HUG AND HOLD ME TIGHT
OR WOULD YOU WALK AWAY
IT ONLY TAKES A LITTLE LOVE
SOME GENTLE CARING TOO
IT DOESN'T COST YOU ANYTHING
SO DO WHAT YOU SHOULD DO
IT'S TIME TO SHARE A LITTLE LOVE
IT'S TIME TO SHOW YOU CARE
I KNOW SOME PEOPLE WILL JUST STOP
AND SOME OF THEM WILL STARE
BUT DOES IT REALLY MATTER
IT'S TIME FOR US TO TEACH
A LITTLE LOVE JUST DOESN'T HURT
AND ISN'T OUT OF REACH
THERE FOR YOU AND THERE FOR ME
THERE FOR EVERYONE
SHOW THE WORLD JUST WHAT TO DO
BEFORE THE CHANCE IS GONE

35. MAYBE

MAYBE IF I SPEAK OUT
MAKE MY THOUGHTS QUITE CLEAR
SOMEONE MIGHT TAKE NOTICE
AND SOMEONE MIGHT JUST HEAR
AND SOMEONE MIGHT JUST LISTEN
TO WHAT I HAVE TO SAY
MAYBE IF I SPEAK OUT
WELL MAYBE JUST TODAY

MAYBE IF I SHOW YOU
THE THINGS I HAVE TO SHOW
PERHAPS YOU'LL UNDERSTAND ME
AND WATCH ME AS I GROW
AND WATCH ME GO THROUGH CHANGES
SLOWLY DAY BY DAY
MAYBE IF I SHOW YOU
WELL MAYBE JUST TODAY

MAYBE IF I SPEAK OUT
SOMEBODY WILL HEAR
I'LL SPEAK OUT VERY SLOWLY
AND VERY LOUD AND CLEAR
AND WHEN I SPEAK I'LL SHOW YOU
THE THINGS IN MY OWN WAY
ONE DAY I MIGHT JUST SHOW YOU
WELL MAYBE NOT TODAY.

36. WATCHING

OUT IN THE WILDS
WHERE THE FOUR WINDS BLOW
WHERE THE RAIN COMES DOWN
IS WHERE I'LL GO
YOU'LL FIND ME THERE
ROAMING FREE
OUT IN THE SUN
IS WHERE I'LL BE

OUT IN THE WILDS
WHERE THE GREEN GRASS GROWS
WHERE THE FLOWERS BLOOM
MY SPIRIT GOES
YOU'LL FIND ME THERE
IN THE PEACE
SITTING UNDER
THE SHADY TREES

OUT IN THE WILDS
FROM THE MORN TIL NIGHT
WHEN THE SUN GOES DOWN
AND THE STARS SHINE BRIGHT
YOU'LL FIND ME THERE
WITH A SIGH
TO WATCH THE WORLD
GO PASSING BY

37. FOLLOWING THE LEADER

IS LIVING AN ILLUSION
JUST A FANTASY
A DREAM OF EVERYTHING WE'D LIKE
AND HOW IT ALL COULD BE
IF DREAMING IS A FANTASY
AND NOT REALITY
DO YOU WISH WHEN YOU AWAKE
IT'S HOW YOUR LIFE COULD BE
DO YOU LIVE THE LIFE YOU CHOOSE
OR CHOSEN JUST FOR YOU
DO YOU DO YOUR OWN THING
OR WHAT THE OTHERS DO
WHEN YOU LET YOUR VOICE BE HEARD
DO YOU SPEAK YOUR MIND
AND WHEN YOU MAKE YOUR OWN WAY
ARE YOU FOLLOWING THE BLIND
IS LIVING AN ILLUSION
A DREAM THAT YOU ONCE HAD
SEE YOURSELF AND BE YOURSELF
AND THEN YOU MIGHT BE GLAD
STOP FOLLOWING THE LEADER
BE JUST WHO YOU ARE
SPEAK YOUR MIND AND SAY IT LOUD
BE BETTER OFF BY FAR.

38. NO TIME FOR REGRET

IF TOMORROW NEVER COMES
WHAT DOES THE FUTURE HOLD
IS THE PAST A MEMORY
NEVER GROWING OLD
TODAY IS LAYING DOWN A PAST
IF ONLY WE ALL KNEW
TODAY WILL LIVE FOREVER
BE SURE OF WHAT YOU DO
CAN WE CHANGE TOMORROW
OR IS IT ALL OUR FATE
IS OUR LIFE LAID OUT FOR US
WE HAVE TO WATCH AND WAIT
ONCE WE LIVE OUR PRESENT
IT THEN BECOMES OUR PAST
IT'S SOMETHING THAT WE CANNOT CHANGE
IT'S SOMETHING THAT WILL LAST
LIVE TODAY AS BEST YOU CAN
IT'S ALL WE'LL EVER GET
ENJOY TODAY AND LIVE IT WELL
WITH NEVER A REGRET.

39. A LITTLE STORY.

I WANT TO TELL A STORY
IT ISN'T VERY LONG
IT HAPPENED LATE ONE WINTER
WHEN WINDS WERE BLOWING STRONG
THE SNOW HAD STARTED FALLING
THE AIR WAS FEELING COLD
I WAS WALKING HOMEWARD BOUND
THE DAY WAS GROWING OLD
I NOTICED SOMETHING MOVING
THROUGH THE CORNER OF MY EYE
I STOPPED TO TAKE A CLOSER LOOK
I COULDN'T PASS ON BY
TWO LITTLE EYES WERE PEEPING OUT
LOOKING QUITE AFRAID
I REACHED MY HAND OUT SLOWLY
AND CONTACT HAD BEEN MADE
THE LITTLE BIRD WAS INJURED
AND LOOKING RATHER FRAIL
I STROKED IT'S HEAD AND BODY
AND THEN IT'S FEATHERED TAIL
I CRADLED IT IN MY WARM HANDS
AND HEADED BACK MY WAY
I WANTED TO TAKE CARE OF IT
AND HELP IT ON ITS WAY
I PUT IT IN A LITTLE BOX
BEFORE I WENT TO SLEEP
IT SAT THERE VERY PEACEFULLY
AND NEVER MADE A CHEEP
IT LOOKED AT ME WITH SADDENED EYES
AND SOMEHOW I JUST KNEW
AND IN THE MORNING WHEN I WOKE
I KNEW JUST WHAT TO DO
I WENT INTO THE GARDEN
AND DUG A LITTLE HOLE
AND LAID TO REST SO PEACEFULLY
THIS GENTLE LITTLE SOUL

40. SUNRISE…SUNSET…

FROM SUNRISE IN THE MORNING
TO SUNSET WHEN IT'S NIGHT
I KNOW THAT I WILL ALWAYS HAVE
NATURE IN MY SIGHT
THE BEAUTY OF THE MORNING SKY
ABOVE THE FIELDS AND TREES
ACROSS THE STREAMS AND RIVERS
DOWN TO THE SHORES AND SEAS
I STAND IN AWE AND WONDER
AT ALL WITHIN MY VIEW
AND EACH TIME THAT I SEE IT
I'M SEEING SOMETHING NEW
AND EVEN IN THE EVENING LIGHT
IN EVERYTHING I SEE
THERE IS A DIFFERENT BEAUTY
LAID OUT IN FRONT OF ME

41. MY STORY

I'VE WALKED DOWN MEMORY LANE BEFORE
I'LL WALK DOWN ONCE AGAIN
SOMETIMES IT BRINGS ME HAPPINESS
SOME DAYS IT BRINGS ME PAIN
REMEMBERING THE OLD TIMES
THE FACES I ONCE KNEW
PLACES THAT I ONCE LIVED
THINGS I USED TO DO
THE LANE CAN BE QUITE NARROW
BUT ALWAYS VERY LONG
SOMETIMES I NEED MY COURAGE
AND HAVE TO BE QUITE STRONG
TO WANDER BACK DOWN MEMORY LANE
AND FACE MY HISTORY
STORIES LAID DOWN THROUGH THE YEARS
THE STORY THAT IS ME

42. MIRROR IMAGE

I LOOKED IN THE MIRROR
AND WHAT DID I SEE?
SOMEBODY STRANGE
WAS LOOKING AT ME
I WASN'T QUITE SURE
JUST WHO I SAW
BUT I KNOW I LOCKED
THE BATHROOM DOOR
THE FACE OF A STRANGER
WAS LOOKING AT ME
I TURNED AROUND QUICK
WHO COULD IT BE?
NO ONE WAS THERE
I WAS ALONE
THE BATHROOM WAS EMPTY
THE PERSON HAD GONE
I LOOKED IN THE MIRROR
AND ONCE AGAIN SAW
A FACE UNFAMILIAR
LOOKING ONCE MORE
I STARTED TO SMILE
IT SMILED BACK AT ME
THIS PERSON SEEMED FRIENDLY
BUT WHO COULD IT BE?
IT TOOK ME A WHILE
AND I LOOKED ONCE MORE
AND THAT'S WHEN I REALISED
JUST WHO I SAW
LOOKING AT ME
AND WEARING A SMILE
SOMETHING I'D NOT SEEN
FOR QUITE A WIIILE
ONE GRINNING FACE
LOOKING SO FREE
RELAXED AND SO HAPPY
YES IT WAS ME.

43. TOP SECRET

IS THIS THE TIME FOR ME TO SAY
WHAT IS ON MY MIND?
OR SHOULD I JUST SAY NOTHING
KEEP PLAYING DUMB AND BLIND?
UNFORTUNATELY I WASN'T DEAF
AND I HEARD EVERY WORD
SOME OF THEM WERE STUPID
AND SOME WERE QUITE ABSURD
I WON'T REPEAT A SINGLE THING
MY LIPS WILL STAY QUITE SEALED
UNLESS IT'S YOU SAYS SOMETHING
THEN ALL WILL BE REVEALED
I'M NOT THE ONE FOR GOSSIP
AND NOT FOR TELLING LIES
BUT WHAT I HEARD AND WHAT I SAW
WAS WITH MY EARS AND EYES
BUT IF ONE DAY IT COMES OUT
EVERYTHING I HEARD
I KNOW THAT IT WILL NOT BE ME
WHO SAID A SINGLE WORD

44. IN SHADES OF GREEN

DID YOU EVER REALISE
HOW MANY SHADES OF GREEN
THERE ARE OUT IN THE COUNTRYSIDE
JUST WAITING TO BE SEEN
THERE'S DIFFERENT SHADES OF GREEN IN GRASS
AND DIFFERENT SHADES IN TREES
AND EVEN THEN THEY CHANGE THEIR HUES
WHEN DANCING IN THE BREEZE
SOME ARE BRIGHT AND SOME ARE DARK
BUT ALL ARE SHADES OF GREEN
SO DID YOU EVER REALISE
HOW MANY CAN BE SEEN?

45. SO IT SEEMS

IT SEEMS TO ME THAT WHEN
I WANT TO MAKE A DIFFERENT CHOICE
NO ONE EVER REALLY WANTS TO
LISTEN TO MY VOICE
I SPEAK OUT LOUD AND CLEARLY
TO MAKE MYSELF BE HEARD
BUT IT SEEMS TO ME THAT NO ONE
EVER HEARS A SINGLE WORD

IT SEEMS TO ME THAT PEOPLE
CANNOT REALLY SEE ME HERE
AS PEOPLE LOOK RIGHT THROUGH ME
ALTHOUGH I'M STANDING NEAR
IT DOESN'T SEEM TO MATTER IF
I EVEN SCREAM AND SHOUT
THEY DO NOT EVEN NOTICE IF
I WAVE MY ARMS ABOUT

IT SEEMS TO ME THAT TALKING
IS JUST A WASTE OF TIME
I'LL JUST GET RIGHT ON LIVING
AND TAKE JUST WHAT IS MINE
IT SEEMS TO ME THAT NO ONE
REALLY EVER CARES
THEY'RE TOO WRAPPED UP AND BLINKERED
WITH ONLY WHAT IS THEIRS.

46. WHAT IS IT ?

I HAVE LOOKED AND I HAVE SEARCHED
BUT STILL I HAVEN'T FOUND
LOOKING HIGH AND SEARCHING LOW
AND EVERYWHERE AROUND
WHAT IT IS I'M LOOKING FOR
I STILL DON'T REALLY KNOW
BUT I WILL KEEP ON SEARCHING
I'M SURE THAT IT WILL SHOW
I'VE LOOKED AROUND THE CORNERS
AND SEARCHED BENEATH THE TREES
BUT STILL I HAVEN'T FOUND IT
WHEN I'VE BEEN UPON MY KNEES
ONE DAY WHEN I'M NOT LOOKING
WHEN MY SEARCHING HAS BEEN DONE
IT WILL BE THERE IN FRONT OF ME
A SINGLE LONELY ONE

47. WHERE IS THE LOVE?

THERE'S LIFE OUT THERE
THAT'S RUSHING BY
I'M HEARING A SHOUT
AND HEARING A CRY
THERE'S FIGHTING AND WAR
WORLD DEVASTATION
PEOPLE FIGHT PEOPLE
NO COMMUNICATION
WHERE IS THE LOVE?
WHY ALL THE HATE?
WHERE IS THE LOVE?
WHERE…?

48. CLOUDS

I WATCH AS CLOUDS
GO DRIFTING BY
FLOATING IN
A BRIGHT BLUE SKY
CLOUDS SO WHITE
A HINT OF GREY
HANGING THERE
THROUGHOUT THE DAY
DRIFTING, FLOATING
IN A SPACE
SLOWLY MOVING
WITH SUCH GRACE
DIFFERENT SHAPES
A DIFFERENT HUE
A CHANGING SHAPE
COMES INTO VIEW
WHO WILL WATCH
THE CLOUDS GO BY
FLOATING IN
A BRIGHT BLUE SKY

49. HALF AND HALF

HALF THE WORLD WAS SLEEPING
HALF THE WORLD AWAKE
HALF THE WORLD IS STARVING
THE REST IS EATING CAKE
HALF THE WORLD IS SMILING
HALF IS SHEDDING TEARS
HALF THE WORLD HAS NEVER CARED
THROUGHOUT ALL THE YEARS
HALF THE WORLD HAS EVERYTHING
HALF THE WORLD HAS NOUGHT
HALF THE WORLD NOW LIVES IN GREED
WITH EVERYTHING IT'S BOUGHT
HALF THE WORLD STILL FEELS NO SHAME
HALF THE WORLD WON'T CARE
HALF THE WORLD JUST KEEPS IT ALL
AND SIMPLY WILL NOT SHARE
HALF THE WORLD JUST DOESN'T HEAR
HALF THE WORLD STAYS BLIND
HALF THE WORLD PLAYS IGNORANT
SO THIS IS HUMANKIND.

50. SOMEONE…

SOMEONE STOPPED MY EYES FROM CRYING
SOMEONE DRIED MY TEARS
BROUGHT A SMILE BACK TO MY FACE
CHASED AWAY MY FEARS
THE LONELY DAYS AND LONELY NIGHTS
WERE SOON LEFT IN THE PAST
BRIGHTER DAYS WERE FILLED WITH LAUGHTER
KNOWING THEY WOULD LAST
TOMORROW TO LOOK FORWARD TO
A JOY TO CELEBRATE
A CHANCE TO MAKE UP FOR LOST TIME
BEFORE IT IS TOO LATE
SOMEONE LIFTED ME FROM DARKNESS
SOMEONE GAVE ME LIGHT
GAVE ME HOPE AND HAPPINESS
A FUTURE THAT IS BRIGHT

51. JUST A LITTLE HELPS

IF ONLY HALF THE WORLD JUST KNEW
WHAT IT'S ALL ABOUT
WHAT OTHERS HAVE TO SUFFER
WOULD THEY STILL HAVE DOUBT?
WOULD THEY GIVE A HELPING HAND?
A SHOULDER JUST TO SHARE
IF ONLY FOR A MINUTE
TO JUST SHOW THAT THEY CARE?
WOULD THEY REACH THEIR POCKETS
AND GIVE AWAY THEIR CHANGE
JUST A LITTLE HELPS A LOT
WHY DOES IT SEEM SO STRANGE
NOT EVERYONE'S AS FORTUNATE
IN THEIR HEALTH OR LIFE
SPARE A THOUGHT FOR THOSE IN NEED
WHO STRUGGLE WITH THEIR STRIFE
THERE BUT FOR THE VERY GRACE
COULD GO YOU OR I
SPARE A THOUGHT FOR ALL OF THEM
AND LISTEN TO THEIR CRY.

52. SHOPPING

ISN'T IT AMAZING
WHAT A BIG SURPRISE
THE KINDS OF THINGS THAT PEOPLE WANT
WHAT ANYBODY BUYS
YOU MAY NOT WANT THAT ORNAMENT
TO YOU IT MAY BE TAT
BUT SOMEONE ELSE MAY TREASURE
A LITTLE THIS OR THAT
SOME PEOPLE GIVE SOME PEOPLE TAKE
OTHERS COME TO BUY
SOME EVEN COME AND GET SOME THINGS
AND DO NOT EVEN TRY
EVERY LITTLE THING THAT'S SOLD
HELPS ALONG THE WAY
WHY NOT COME ALONG AND BROWSE
ON YOUR SHOPPING DAY

53. WINTER WASHING BLUES

DO YOU REMEMBER WASHING
ON THOSE COLD AND WINTER DAYS?
YOU HUNG YOUR WASHING ON THE LINE
IN THE MISTY HAZE
IT DIDN'T TAKE THAT VERY LONG
BEFORE YOUR CLOTHES TURNED WHITE
AND HUNG THERE STIFF AND SOLID
IN THE MID-DAY LIGHT
IT DIDN'T EVEN MATTER
HOW MUCH THE SUN WOULD SHINE
YOUR CLOTHES STAYED FROZEN SOLID
ON THE WASHING LINE
HOUR BY HOUR THINGS HUNG THERE
YOU KNEW THERE'D BE NO CHANGE
AND YET YOU LEFT IT HANGING
YOU DIDN'T THINK IT STRANGE
AND AS THE LIGHT WAS FADING
YOU WENT BACK OUT ONCE MORE
LIFTED DOWN YOUR WASHING
YOUR BASKET ON THE FLOOR
YOU COULDN'T FOLD THE WASHING
THE SITUATION DIRE
YOU PUT IT ON A CLOTHES HORSE
BESIDE A ROARING FIRE!

54. DIFFERENCES.

WHY DON'T PEOPLE OF THE WORLD
SEE THROUGH DIFFERENT EYES
HEAR THE DIFFERENT THINGS I HEAR
THE HELLO'S AND GOODBYES
SPOKEN IN A DIFFERENT VOICE
THE MEANING IS THE SAME
WE EACH OF US ARE DIFFERENT
YET LIVE BY THE SAME NAME
WE NEED TO LIVE IN HARMONY
WE NEED TO LIVE IN PEACE
PUT ASIDE OUR DIFFERENCES
HOSTILITIES MIGHT CEASE
WHAT IS IT MAKES THE WORLD GO ROUND
GIVES LIFE VARIETY
ALL THE DIFFERENCES WE HAVE
HOW CAN IT REALLY BE?
ACCEPT EACH OTHER'S DIFFERENCES
AND STILL PUT THEM ASIDE
LIVE TOGETHER PEACEFULLY
AND LIVE LIFE SIDE BY SIDE.

55. TIME.

AGE MAY NOT BE EASY
TIME WILL MAKE ITS MARK
IT CREEPS UP ON US SLOWLY
A THIEF FROM OUT THE DARK
IT ROBS US OF OUR CHILDHOOD
AND ROBS US OF OUR YOUTH
WE MAY NOT LIKE THE THINGS WE GET
BUT WHAT WE GET IS TRUTH
THE LINES THAT SHOW OUR CHARACTER
ALSO SHOW OUR AGE
THEY'RE THERE FOR ANYONE TO READ
LIKE LINES UPON A PAGE
TIME WILL TAKE OUR INNOCENCE
BUT MAY NOT MAKE US WISE
TIME WILL GIVE US HINDSIGHT
WE CANNOT SEE THROUGH EYES
TIME WILL GIVE US LOTS OF ACHES
AND TIME WILL BRING US PAIN
IT ALSO BRINGS US SUNSHINE
TO CHASE AWAY THE RAIN
WE CANNOT STOP THE TICK OF TIME
AND THINGS THAT IT CAN DO
TIME HAS ALWAYS BEEN HERE
YET TIME IS ALWAYS NEW

56. PEOPLE, PEOPLE EVERYWHERE.

ALL THOSE DIFFERENT PEOPLE
WALKING ON THE STREET
I WONDER WHERE THEY'RE GOING
I WONDER WHO THEY'LL MEET?
WHAT'S THEIR DESTINATION
WHERE IS IT THEY'VE BEEN
WHAT IS IT THEY'RE DOING
I WONDER WHAT THEY'VE SEEN
ARE THESE PEOPLE HAPPY
ARE THESE PEOPLE SAD
WHAT IS IT THEY'RE WANTING
OR WHAT IS IT THEY'VE HAD
LIFE CAN BE A MYSTERY
THEY'RE ACTORS IN A PLAY
I SEE THEM OUT THERE ALL THE TIME
I WATCH THEM EVERY DAY.

57. WHAT IF…?

IF I HAD A PENNY
FOR EVERY LITTLE THOUGHT
WOULD I BE A RICH MAN
OR WOULD I STILL HAVE NOUGHT?
IF I HAD A WISH
FOR EVERY FALLING STAR
WOULD I HAVE MY HEARTS DESIRE
OR STILL BE LOOKING FAR?
IF I PICKED A SMALL PIN
FROM LYING ON THE FLOOR
WOULD I GET SOME GOOD LUCK
OR SIMPLY HAVE NO MORE?
WHAT IF THESE AND SO MUCH MORE
COULD REALLY CHANGE MY WORLD
SHOULD I, COULD I, WOULD I
AS MY LIFE UNFURLED

58. THE LADIES WHO LUNCH.

THERE'S TWO OR THREE OR EVEN FIVE
WHO MEET UP ONCE A WEEK
THEY SOMETIMES MEET FOR COFFEE
A CHANCE FOR THEM TO SPEAK
AT OTHER TIMES THEY HAVE THEIR LUNCH
THEY EAT AND HAVE A CHAT
SPENDING TIME TO TALK ABOUT
A LITTLE THIS AND THAT.
SOMETIMES THEY PUT THE WORLD TO RIGHTS
SOMETIMES THEY'LL DISAGREE
AND THEN THEY'LL GOSSIP ALL ABOUT
THE THINGS THAT THEY MIGHT SEE
A LITTLE LAUGH JUST NOW AND THEN
A GIGGLE THEY SUPPRESS
A SMILE A WAVE THEN TALK ABOUT
SOMEBODY ELSE'S DRESS
ONE IS LEADER OTHERS LED
THE GROUPS WILL STAY THE SAME
THEY KEEP ON MEETING WEEK BY WEEK
AND ONLY HAVE ONE AIM
TO CATCH UP ON THE RUMOURS
THE GOSSIP AND THE CHAT
AND "MY GOODNESS DID YOU EVER SEE
THAT WOMAN'S DREADFUL HAT!"

59. THIS IS ME…

IF I COULD TURN BACK HANDS OF TIME
I DON'T THINK THAT I WOULD
IT WOULDN'T BE OF ANY USE
AND WOULDN'T DO ME GOOD
I'VE LIVED MY LIFE THE BEST I CAN
AND YES I'VE MADE MISTAKES
I'VE BEEN THROUGH GOOD TIMES AND SOME BAD TIMES
HAD SOME LUCKY BREAKS
I'VE SMILED A LOT AND CRIED A LOT
AND REALLY LAUGHED OUT LOUD
DONE THINGS I DO NOT TALK ABOUT
AND THINGS OF WHICH I'M PROUD
I'VE TRIED MY BEST TO DO MY BEST
IN EVERY WAY I CAN
THAT'S WHY TODAY THAT I CAN SAY
I AM A REAL TRUE MAN

60. DEATH OF A HUNDRED YEARS

IF A TREE FALLS IN THE WIND
DOES ANYBODY SEE
DOES ANYBODY FEEL IT'S PAIN
OF WHAT IT'S LIKE TO BE
DOES ANYBODY EVER HEAR
ITS LOUD YET SILENT CRY
AS IT CRASHES TO THE FLOOR
TO WHERE IT'S GOING TO DIE
WITH BROKEN BRANCHES ALL ABOUT
AND ROOTS RIPPED FROM THE GROUND
IT LIES THERE IN A SHATTERED STATE
NO MORE TO MAKE A SOUND
NO LEAVES TO RUSTLE IN THE WIND
NO LONGER BRANCHES SWAY
NO PLACE FOR BIRDS TO MAKE A NEST
OR REST BOTH NIGHT AND DAY
DOES ANYBODY NOTICE?
DOES ANYBODY CARE?
A TREE THAT ONCE GREW MANY YEARS
NO LONGER STANDS JUST THERE

61. THE LIFT

WHEN SUN SHINES ON THE MEADOW
AND CLOUDS DESERT THE SKY
THE BRIGHTNESS OF A WILDFLOWER
WILL ALWAYS CATCH MY EYE
THE GRASS WILL SEEM MUCH GREENER
WHEN LIT UP BY THE SUN
THE DAY WILL SEEM MUCH BRIGHTER
WITH ALL THE DARK CLOUDS GONE
THE BIRDSONG WILL BE LOUDER
THE BEES WILL COME AROUND
AND BUTTERFLIES WILL JUST GO BY
WITHOUT A SINGLE SOUND
THE WIND WILL TURN INTO A BREEZE
AND WHISPER THROUGH THE LAND
SUMMER IS A JOY TO HAVE
SO TAKE IT BY THE HAND
AND WANDER THROUGH A MEADOW
WALK BENEATH THE TREES
LISTEN TO THE BIRDSONG
AND WATCH THE BUSY BEES
FEEL THE SUN UPON YOUR FACE
AND WATCH AS CLOUDS DRIFT BY
ENJOY ANOTHER SUMMER DAY
AND LET IT LIFT YOU HIGH

62. STARS OF MEMORIES

LIKE THE STARS THAT TWINKLE
EACH AND EVERY NIGHT
MEMORIES ARE OUT OF REACH
BUT NEVER OUT OF SIGHT.
EACH IS A REMINDER
THAT THINGS ARE NOT SO DARK
EACH A POINT OF BRIGHTNESS
JUST LIKE A LITTLE SPARK
THEY GIVE US HOPE AND COMFORT
IN A TIME OF NEED
THEY HEAL OUR HEARTS OF OPEN PAIN
EVEN WHEN THEY BLEED
MEMORIES ARE TREASURES
JUST LIKE THE STARS AT NIGHT
PRECIOUS AND QUITE PRICELESS
AND ALWAYS SHINING BRIGHT.

63. YOUNG AND FREE

TELL ME WHY SHOULD I GROW UP
AND WHY SHOULD I GROW OLD
LET ME DO JUST WHAT I PLEASE
AND NOT WHAT I AM TOLD
I LIKE MY MAD BEHAVIOUR
I LIKE TO ACT THE FOOL
SOMEONE SHOW ME WHERE IT'S WRIT
LET ME SEE THE RULE
I MAY NOT BE SO YOUNG NOW
AS NUMBERS START TO RISE
I STILL LOOK AT THE WORLD OUTSIDE
THROUGH A YOUNGSTERS EYES
MY ACTIONS MAY LOOK FOOLISH
AND SOMETIMES STRANGE AND QUEER
BUT WHO SAYS WHAT IS RIGHT OR WRONG
AND WHAT IS IT THEY FEAR
MY ACTIONS WILL NOT HURT YOU
BUT MAKE ME FEEL QUITE GOOD
THEY MAKE ME FEEL QUITE YOUNG AT HEART
IS THAT UNDERSTOOD?
I WANT TO GROW OLD HAPPY
FEELING YOUNG AND FREE
REMEMBER WHAT I TELL YOU
AND WHAT YOU GET IS ME!

64. COLOURS BECOMING

DID YOU SEE THE SUNSET?
AND THE COLOURS IN THE SKY
THE BEAUTY OF THE EVENING
ALMOST MADE ME CRY
THE SLOWLY CHANGING COLOURS
THE ORANGES AND RED
LIGHTING UP THE NIGHT SKY
HIGH ABOVE MY HEAD

DID YOU SEE THE SUNSET?
AS IT WENT BEHIND THE TREES
OR FALL BEHIND THE HILLSDIE
ACROSS THE CALMEST SEAS
HOWEVER YOU MAY SEE IT
WHEREVER YOU MAY BE
THE GLORY OF A SUNSET
IS A SIGHT THAT YOU SHOULD SEE

DID YOU SEE THE SUNSET?
DID IT CATCH YOUR EYE?
DID YOU LET IT CAPTIVATE YOU?
DID IT PASS YOU BY?
IT DOES NOT HAPPEN EVERY NIGHT
SO WATCH IT WHILE YOU CAN
APPRECIATE ITS BEAUGTY
BECOME A PEACEFUL MAN.

65. CONNECTIONS

DO YOU KNOW JUST WHO IT WAS?
HAVE YOU GOT A CLUE?
WHO IT WAS THAT BUILT THAT HOUSE
THAT ROAD, THAT BRIDGE WHEN NEW
DO YOU EVER THINK ABOUT
WHO MADE THE CLOTHES YOU WEAR?
WHO MADE THE THINGS WITHIN YOUR HOME?
THE THINGS YOU EVEN SHARE
THOSE THINGS THAT STOOD A HUNDRED YEARS
WERE MADE BY SOMEONE TOO
SO DO YOU EVER REALISE
THEY MIGHT HAVE BEEN LIKE YOU
DO YOU EVER THINK ABOUT
THEIR FAMILIES AND THEIR WIVES
THEY MAY HAVE HAD SOME CHILDREN
WHILE LIVING OUT THEIR LIVES
YOU MIGHT NOT EVEN REALISE
CONNECTIONS THERE MIGHT BE
BETWEEN THOSE LONG GONE PEOPLE
CONNECTING YOU AND ME.

66. WHAT A WASTE.

SCATTERED LITTER ON A BEACH
COLLECTING WITH THE STONES
A MASS OF DIRTY PLASTIC
CAUGHT AMONG SOME BONES
LIFE DESTROYED BY HUMANS
SO CARELESS WITH NO THOUGHT
RUBBISH THROWN AWAY ONE DAY
FROM SOMETHING THAT WE BOUGHT
WE MIGHT KNOW THE DIFFERENCE
WHAT IS FOOD OR WASTE
BUT CREATURES LIVING ON THE SEAS
WILL SWALLOW THINGS IN HASTE
CHOKING LIFE FROM OUT THEM
NO RESCUE FROM THEIR FATE
AND IF BY CHANCE WE FIND THEM
TOO OFTEN IT'S TOO LATE
BEFORE WE DROP OUR LITTER
OR THROW THINGS IN THE SEA
JUST THINK OF ALL THE HARM WE CAUSE
TO THE WILD AND FREE
TAKE HOME WHAT WE DO NOT NEED
IT ISN'T HARD TO DO
LET THE WILD STAY LIVING SAFE
WAY OUT THERE IN THE BLUE.

67. FINAL DECISION

IT'S THE FICKLE HAND OF FATE
WHICH DECIDES WHAT YOU WILL DO
IT MIGHT BE SOMETHING OLD
OR IT MIGHT BE SOMETHING NEW
YOU DO NOT MAKE DECISIONS
YOUR CHOICE IS READY DONE
YOU DO WHAT FATE DECIDES FOR YOU
THE SAME FOR EVERYONE
FATE HAS PLANS DRAWN UP FOR YOU
ALTHOUGH YOU THINK YOU'RE FREE
IT DOESN'T MATTER WHAT YOU DO
WHAT WILL BE WILL BE

68. I WHO HAVE NOTHING

SHE'S A LITTLE OLD LADY
SMILES A LOT
HASN'T MUCH
BUT WHAT SHE'S GOT,
SHE'LL SHARE AROUND
WITHOUT A THOUGHT
EVEN GIVE
WHAT SHE'S JUST BOUGHT
NOT MUCH MONEY
HAS GOOD HEALTH
THIS MEANS MORE
THAN LOTS OF WEALTH
SHARES HER LAUGHTER
SHARES A SMILE
ALWAYS GOES
THAT EXTRA MILE
LEARN A LESSON
WHEN YOU SEE
JUST HOW RICH
LIFE CAN BE
WHEN YOU LEARN
THE LESSON TAUGHT
BY LITTLE OLD LADY
WHO HAS NOUGHT.

69. I...

GIVE ME VOICE
SO I CAN SAY
WHAT NEEDS SAYING
DAY BY DAY
GIVE ME EYES
SO I CAN SEE
WHAT THERE IS
IN FRONT OF ME
I HAVE DOUGH
TO MAKE MY BREAD
MAKING SURE
THAT I AM FED
I HAVE DRINK
TO QUENCH MY THIRST
SO NEVER EVER
PUT ME FIRST
I HAVE EVERYTHING
I NEED
I DON'T HAVE WANT
I DON'T HAVE GREED
GIVE TO THOSE
WHO HAVE LESS
AND LIVE THEIR LIVES
IN QUIET DISTRESS

70. THE DANCER

DID IT REALLY HAPPEN?
IS IT REALLY TRUE?
WAS I THAT SO STUPID?
I GUESS I NEVER KNEW
DID ANYBODY SEE ME
AS I TOOK THE FALL
ALL ACROSS THE WOODEN FLOOR
RIGHT INTO THE WALL
I HEARD SOMEBODY LAUGH OUT
I GUESS SOMEBODY SAW
I LIKE TO THINK I TRIPPED UP
I'VE DONE IT ONCE BEFORE
I GUESS I HAVE TWO LEFT FEET
AND I WILL NEVER DANCE
I THROW MY CAUTION TO THE WIND
AND SOMETIMES TAKE A CHANCE
I NEVER LEARN MY LESSON
I SAIL ACROSS THE FLOOR
OFTEN ON MY BOTTOM
LEAVING ME QUITE SORE
I'VE DONE IT ONCE, I'VE DONE IT TWICE
I'LL DO IT YET AGAIN
I CAN'T RESIST THE MUSIC
IT REALLY IS A PAIN
I'LL NEVER BE A DANCER
AS ALL CAN PLAINLY SEE
MY FEET DON'T DO THE THINGS I WANT
YET THEY'RE ATTACHED TO ME
THEY ACT SO INDEPENDENTLY
IT DOESN'T QUITE SEEM QUITE TRUE
I'LL NEVER LEARN MY LESSON
AND IT ISN'T SOMETHING NEW.

71. YESTERDAY, TODAY, TOMORROW

WAITING FOR TOMORROW
BUT TOMORROW'S NEVER HERE
THE PRESENT CAN BE HAZY
AND THE PAST BE VERY CLEAR
WATCHING FOR THE FUTURE
AND WHAT IT JUST MIGHT BRING
THE PRESENT IS NEGLECTED
THE PAST A LONG GONE THING
WE WORRY WHAT WILL HAPPEN
AND DWELL UPON THE PAST
THE PRESENT IS UPON US
AND RUSHES BY TOO FAST
TAKE OUT TIME TO STOP A WHILE
NO MATTER WHERE OR HOW
TOMORROW ISN'T PROMISED
SO APPRECIATE THE NOW

72. IN YOUR CHAIR.

OVER IN THE CORNER
THERE STANDS AN EMPTY CHAIR
MY EYES ARE SLOWLY FILLED WITH TEARS
FOR YOU'RE NOT SITTING THERE
I CANNOT SEEK YOUR WISDOM
OR ASK FOR YOUR ADVICE
I'M SURE I SAW YOU SITTING THERE
MORE THAN ONCE OR TWICE
YOUR CUP NO LONGER HOLDS YOUR TEA
YOUR PLATE SITS ON THE SHELF
YOUR KNIFE AND FORK IS PUT AWAY
I SIT ALL BY MYSELF
I LOOK AROUND AT THESE FOUR WALLS
AND LISTEN FOR YOUR VOICE
AND ALL I HEAR IS SILENCE
A LOUD AND EMPTY NOISE
AT TIMES I LOOK AROUND ME
AND HOPE I'LL SEE YOUR FACE
BUT ALL I SEE IS EMPTINESS
A DARK AND LONELY SPACE
I SIT HERE WITH MY MEMORIES
REMEMBERING WHAT'S PAST
I SIT HERE WITH MY HOPES AND DREAMS
AS TIME GOES BY SO FAST
IT DOESN'T SEEM THAT LONG AGO
THAT YOU WERE SITTING THERE
SPEAKING WORDS OF WISDOM
WHILE SITTING IN YOUR CHAIR

73. APPRECIATION SOCIETY

TWINKLE, TWINKLE LITTLE STAR
SHINING UP ABOVE
REMINDING ME OF NATURE
AND ALL THE THINGS I LOVE
THE LITTLE DAISY IN THE GRASS
CLOUDS UP IN THE SKY
THE SONG I HEAR OF BLACKBIRDS
THE BEES AND BUTTERFLY
A SUNSET IN THE EVENING
A GENTLE COOLING BREEZE
THE FEEL OF GRASS BENEATH MY FEET
THE HIGH AND MIGHTY TREES
WITH WONDERS ALL AROUND ME
I'M GLAD THAT I AM FREE
GLAD I CAN APPRECIATE
THE THINGS I HEAR AND SEE

74. WHAT I'VE GOT?

IF I SHOW YOU WHAT I'VE GOT
WILL YOU SHOW ME YOURS?
THROUGH AN OPEN WINDOW
OR FROM BEHIND CLOSED DOORS
IF YOU PROMISE NOT TO LAUGH
I'LL SHOW YOU RIGHT AWAY
BUT PROMISE NOT TO TOUCH IT
IN THE LIGHT OF DAY
I'M SURE THAT WHEN YOU SEE IT
YOU'LL REALLY BE AMAZED
NO ONE HAS ONE LIKE IT
YOUR MIND WILL BE LEFT DAZED
ITS SIZE IS QUITE AMAZING
BE SURE THAT IT IS REAL
AND IF YOU'LL BE QUITE GENTLE
I'LL LET YOU HAVE A FEEL
BUT ONLY IN THE EVENING
AS NIGHT IS DRAWING NEAR
AND LET ME REASSURE YOU
THERE'S NOTHING YOU NEED FEAR
DON'T ASK ME TO DESCRIBE IT
OR WHAT I USE IT FOR
BUT IF I SHOW YOU WHAT I'VE GOT
YOU'LL WANT TO SEE IT MORE

75. MOBILE LIVES

EVERYBODY'S WALKING ROUND
A PHONE UP TO THE EAR
OR FINGERS TAPPING ON A SCREEN
THEY NEITHER SEE NOR HEAR
THE WORLD THAT'S ALL AROUND THEM
AS LIFE GOES RUSHING BY
THEY HAVE NO TIME TO STOP AND TALK
NO MATTER HOW THEY TRY
WE'RE ALL BECOMING STRANGERS
TO PEOPLE THAT WE SEE
WE KNOW THEIR NUMBERS ON THE PHONE
WHOEVER THEY MAY BE
WE CANNOT PUT THE VOICES
TO FACES WE SHOULD KNOW
WE DO NOT KNOW THE FACES
OF THE PEOPLE ON THE GO
WE'VE ALL BECOME QUITE INSULAR
IN OUR LIVES TODAY
WE LIVE OUR LIVES BY MOBILE PHONES
IS THIS THE MODERN WAY?
THE MODERN WAY TO LIVE OUR LIVES
THE MODERN WAY TO BE
WITH LITTLE CONVERSATIONS
AND NO COMMUNITY.

www.ingramcontent.com/pod-product-compliance
Lightning Source LLC
LaVergne TN
LVHW022112080426
835511LV00007B/775